Literature written for young adults...

by young adults.

Allow yourself to be surprised.

Letters from the Underground
Young Writers Chapbook Series

Ever Taylor

Atlanta

Copyright © 2013 by Ever Taylor
Published by VerbalEyze Press

All rights reserved. Printed in the United States of America. No part of this book may be used or reproduced in any manner whatsoever, including Internet usage, without written permission from VerbalEyze Press except in the case of brief quotations embodied in critical articles and reviews.

Cover art © 2013 by Susan Arauz Barnes
Editing by Derek Koehl and Tavares Stephens
ISBN: 978-0-9856451-5-1

VerbalEyze Press books are available at special discounts for bulk purchases in the United States by corporations, institutions and other organizations.

For information, address VerbalEyze Press, 1376 Fairbanks Street SW, Atlanta, Georgia 30310.

VerbalEyze does not participate, endorse, or have any authority or responsibility concerning private correspondence between our authors and the public. All mail addressed to authors are forwarded, but the publisher cannot, unless specifically instructed by the author, give out an address or phone number.

VerbalEyze Press
A division of VerbalEyze, Inc.
www.verbaleyze.org

I definitely want to thank my parents
for never giving up on me,
no matter how unrealistic my dreams are.
I love you for that.
– Ever

Table of Contents

Foreword 11
Editors' Note 13
I Am From 15
Battling Beauty 19
Why 23
Give a Boy a Gun 27
Tag 31
Forever Must Be Short 35
How I Loved Your Eyes 39
13 Views of Darkness 45
A Letter from the Underground 49

Letters from the Underground

Foreword

Many a black and white speckled notebook has been privy to the growing pains of young artists. They sketch, narrate, poet and rhyme to make sense of the world and orient themselves to the gravitational pull of coming of age. But their musings beg for answers and an empathetic head nod, so YaHeard? Poetics was born.

Whether speaking heartache at the mic, spitting social commentary over tracks or texting observations into the ether, the power and influence of word is undeniable and YaHeard? Poets study the craft, explore their creative process and learn how to promote their artistic endeavors through collaborations with organizations like VerbalEyze, a beacon for young artists.

YaHeard? was founded by Educator-Artists to support the creative stirrings of tweens and teens and the publication of this chapbook honors and encourages the work of a young artists whose passion and talent confirms them as part of a new generation of prolific writers, artists and musicians. Their musings have escaped from first notebooks and into your hands. Answer if you dare; head nod if you must ---this young scribe dares to explore the power of voice.

Ya Heard?

Susan Arauz Barnes
Co-founder, YaHeard? Poetics

Editors' Note

The Young Writers Chapbook Series is an expression of the mission and vision that is core to what we do at VerbalEyze. Through this series, we are able to provide talented, emerging young authors their debut introduction to the reading public. We are grateful that you also share an enthusiasm for young authors and the vibrant and energized perspectives they bring to our shared understanding of the human experience and what it means to live, love, long, lose and wonder as we travel together through this world.

We are pleased to bring to you an exceptional young writer, Ever Taylor, with this edition of the Young Writers Chapbook. We trust that you will be as engaged and challenged by her words as we have been. Ever is part of an exceptional group of young writers, YaHeard? Poetics. She and her fellow writers are an never-ending encouragement and inspiration to us.

Read, enjoy and, as always, *allow yourself to be surprised*.

Derek Koehl
Tavares Stephens

I Am From

I am from

The red splatter

On the side of apartment 306

I am from

Listening to Ant Terry

At every family reunion

"She betta not talk to me like that,"

"Who da h…heck she think she is."

That nosey old woman

I am from

Chicken,

Mac and cheese

Sweet potato pie

Every Sunday dinner

Aromas dancing in and out my nostrils

I am from

My warm

Cozy

Soft like a cloud in the light blue sky

Pony Doll

My only friend

Young Writers Chapbook Series

I am from

My inspiration box

It hides my secrets

It tells my story

Ever Taylor

Battling Beauty

As I glance

At this huge animal

In the mirror

As I cry

Tears tumble down like gumdrops

My spirit crumbles

I feel hollow

As I lie

You are beautiful

Stabbing it into my soul

In disbelief

In the mirror

As I cry

Tears tumble down like gumdrops

My spirit crumbles

I feel hollow

As I lie

You are beautiful

Stabbing it into my soul

In disbelief

As I look

Into those big brown eyes
I see a past
Scars others placed on my self-worth
The one on my heart
May never heal
As I whisper
I'm sorry
Forgiving me
Letting myself be loved
Allowing love of self
Unlocking the chains on my heart
I am free

Ever Taylor

Why

If life is so lucky
Why do we come out of our mothers' wombs crying?
Why is America the richest country in the world?
If we still owe trillions of dollars to China
Why does an athlete's dinner cost more than someone's yearly salary?
Why do girls play with Barbie's for the first 10 years of their lives?
And try to be like them the next 10?
Why clean the streets if people are just going to mess them up again?
Why fix the Ozone layer if we would be dead and gone by the time it breaks
Why does love hurt
And
Pain feel so good?
Why do people formulate stereotypes without proof?
Why do Americans not realize that the colors on the flag represent
Red blood slaves shed to make this country a true democracy
Blue bruises the slave owners beat into them that gave them

strength
And white people who got credit for it

Why must I say no offense after that line?
Why did it take 40 years after the civil right movement for there to be a black president?
Why do Blacks and Latinos think that they fought two different struggles?
Why don't people realize that immigrants built this country?
Why is silence so loud?
Why am I told to pipe down when I am telling the truth?
Why do we call boys men if they still act like children?
Why do parents believe kids listen to do as I say/
Not as I do?
Why are females looked at as being weaker than males if
Males lift weights
And
Women lift sons
Why must we destroy one thing to create something else?
Why do men beat women?
Why do women tear down men?
Why do people give up on their dreams?
Why must people die to save a life?
Why does it take death for brilliance to be recognized?
Why does history repeat itself?

Ever Taylor

Why is the most constant thing in life change
If ain't nothing changed but the date?
Why do artists fall from stardom?
Why isn't hip- hop fun anymore?
Why do mysteries exist?
Why didn't you mention my monthly's friends?
Crampy and Bloaty
Why do parents hide truths from their children?
Why did every other person have a hard childhood?
If life is so lucky
Why did we come out our mothers' wombs crying?

Give a Boy a Gun

Give a boy a whip

He'll beat a man

Long lashes

Hot flashes

Black

Blue

Brown

Skin dripping of red rain

Cloud of bloody fist

Whip him to his knees

But

He'll never lay flat

He is strong

Not a slave

But

An enslaved African

Someday he knows his children will be free

Give a boy a war

He'll kill a soldier

Gun

Powder

Young Writers Chapbook Series

Loud

Fire

Fierce eyes

Pained hearts

Last cannon fired

Battle ain't over

Give a boy a rope

He'll suffocate the life

Out of a revolutionary

No Negroes Allowed

Pickett signs

Voices cry

Strange fruit

Hanging on the trees

White hoods

Dark minds

Another great tree

Fallen

Give a boy his-story

He'll repeat it

Walking down a dark and empty street

BANG!

Skittles scattered across the sidewalk

Red mixed with Arizona tea

Give man strength

Ever Taylor

He will become a leader

Microphone

Suit

Standing tall

I Have a Dream

A bullet took his life

Not the dream

Give a boy a gun

He'll leave a legacy for a man

Tag

I rated you a 1,000 on a scale from 1 to 10

I've loved you since

I was 5

When you racing me to the sand box

Made my heart beat as fast as it did

When we played hide and seek

Anxiously waiting for you to find me

Just so I could feel your touch against

Skin tanned from playing out in the sun for so long

No sunscreen to smooth away the loneliness I felt

When I couldn't hear your footsteps anymore

I would peak from behind the thorny bush

YOU'RE IT!

When I

Found you

You were crouching down behind a tree

A splinter in your palm

As much as I wanted to help you

I didn't know how

And it broke my heart

More than the sadness I felt when I realized our game was over

Even though we've both grown up
Your mocha eyes
Still make me melt
Like my favorite flavor of ice cream
Two scoops of coffee with caramel syrup
Your caramel skin must have tasted sweet when the sun kissed it
Love never tasted the same after you
I still remember my first kiss
A summer midnight
You were sleeping over 'cause your mom had to work late
Watching Spiderman in my brother's room
You were my Peter Parker
I was your Mary Jane
Imagining we were kissing in the rain
I didn't want to pull away
It frightened me
Like the time the fire alarm went off
When I cooked our popcorn too long
Opening the microwave
Smoke emerging through the door
The kitchen so small that it covered the entire room
When you heard me coughing
Your hand touched mine
I knew you would find me

Ever Taylor

You always found me
Would always pick me
When we played duck-duck-goose
And I will always choose you to chase after
My eyes told you more than my own reflection told me
I still remember crying in your arms
My tears drops a pattern on your shirt
Never mind what I was crying about
You just wanted to love the pain away
When you moved away
I cursed the sea that separated us
My dreams were filled with the games we used to play
When you came back
I had this fantasy that it was for me
You found me
My love for you runs deeper than any of the childhood games
    we played
When you read this
Let the words find their way to your heart
Like I let you find me
Tag,
You're it

Forever Must Be Short

I remember when there was a time
You couldn't take your eyes off me
Now
You can't even gaze in my direction
Why
Why is it so hard for you to feel?
To touch
To hold me
Anymore
Let my words sink into you
My voice a memory of how wonderful God is
My tears make you crumble to your knees
'Cause you can't bare the sight of me crying
You used to love me
You used to be my Clyde
And I was your Bonnie

Now
I'm your Tina
And
You're my Ike

'Cause your silence feels like punches

Pounding against my heart

My heart

My heart pounding when you walk by

Anxious

Hoping one day

Your eyes could meet mine once again

Like they did when our love was

Innocent

New

And

Golden

Used to get high off your laugh

Now

I'm having withdrawals of your smile

I'll wait for you

As my heart cracks

I'll wait for you

Forever must be short

'Cause that's how long you said you would love me

Ever Taylor

How I Loved Your Eyes

If only for a gaze

I could see you

For the last

Time

Moments

Seconds

Of our lives together

Your deep brown eyes

Oh, how I loved your eyes

Your dark complexion

Against the

Red and blue

Lights flashing

Loudly

Behind you

Red and blue

Skin before you

My body lay

Dormant

Still

Calm

Quiet
For the first time
Since I met you
Your
Deep
Brown
Eyes
How much lie behind them
Black
Poisonous
Tears of sorrow
Streamed down your face
Why must you cry?
When it's too late for tears
Your eyes
Deep
Dark
Malicious
Eyes
I've fallen
Into your trap
Trance
You have hypnotized me
Stripped me of my
Dignity

Ever Taylor

Innocence

Sanity

Your eyes

Hollow

As they whisk you away

Wear your silver bracelets with pride

And your orange jumpsuit with honor

Remember me

Us

You

You did this

Your eyes

Remorseful

Loving

Caring

As you watch the blood ooze from my mouth

My eyes

Swollen shut

Blue

Black bruises

Across my

Soft

High

Cheek bones

With two fists

Young Writers Chapbook Series

You took my last breath
My last words
I love you
The least you can do is say goodbye
As they force you into the
Big
Black car
Your eyes
Deep
Brown
Eyes
Blood shot red
You whisper
I love you too
Oh, how I will miss your eyes

Ever Taylor

13 Views of Darkness

I.

Midnight figures

Following

Watching my every move

II.

Fear

Seen

In my eyes

III.

Screams linger

Hopping from

One wall to the other

In one ear

Out the other

IV.

Loss of direction

Loss of control

Loss of concern

V.

Captured

Enclosed

Imprisoned

VI.

Consumed

In loneliness

Filled with tears

VII.

Droplets of water

Falling from our rusty facet

Heard

VIII.

Shades of black

Or

Shades of blue

IX.

Inspiration

Trapped

In the dark

X.

Silence fell

Midnight has come

XI.

Freedom

Exhale

XII.

Kissed by an icy chill

I awaken in black

XIII.

The night star

Has risen

A Letter from the Underground

Dear Society,

I have never been to

Zoo Atlanta

Or

Fern bank

But I live in the jungle

                        Waking up

Not knowing whether my life would abruptly end

Due to someone's bad aim

Was all the wildlife I needed

I have never seen Annie

Wizard of Oz

Or

Toy Story

                        In my story

Toys killed

The only wizard I knew was my dad

He always found a way to disappear

It ain't no hard knock life for me

I just call it survival

My only idols were innocent criminals

You know the ones that robbed 5 banks

Had 10 counts of trespassing

And 15 counts of public indecency

For sagging their pants so low

They wrote songs about it

But I still wore shirts

Embroidered with spray-paint

And a picture of their emotionlessly serious faces

Screaming,

FREE TAY-TAY!

'Cause he was a father to me

I've never seen X-Factor

Or

American Idol

                The stars of my neighborhood were people
                who dared to rock the MIC

They would

Spit a little rhyme

And have a little time

To feel like something

To let the light shine

'Cause there's a thin line

Between good and divine

And time flew by

So

Fast

Ever Taylor

That you forgot that you might

Never leave the block

Without a mic or a ball

But who says I wanted to

I have never been to space

But I see astronauts

In my neighborhood

Who get high to kill their lows

But with every blow

They sink deeper into their sorrows

They push dream out of bellowing nostrils

And they evaporate into gray clouds

Their silence is loud

A mere breath is a shout

A cry for help

Never heard inside a prison cell

While daddy's in jail

Mom sells her body

Just to keep a fork full of Ramen to our mouths

Even though I don't smile as much as the kids on the Sunny D commercials

My value brand juice was sweet enough for me

       Sincerely Yours,
       DGK
       Dirty Ghetto Kids

Ever Taylor started writing at the age of eight, and her main inspiration were artists like Erykah Badu and Lauryn Hill. They showed her that she could incorporate her singing with her poetry. She finds inspiration in music. She likes to write about all that goes unsaid. To have fun, she reads to her niece and nephew. They push her to never stop believing because if she does not follow her dreams, it will teach them that they cannot go after their own dreams.

Photo credit: arauzingink

Empowering young writers to say, **"I am my scholarship!"**

Open call for submissions to the *Young Writers Anthology*!

See your work in print!

    Become a published writer!

        **Earn royalites that can help
you pay for college!s**

VerbalEyze Press is accepting submissions from young adult writers, ages 13 to 22, in any of the following genres:

- poetry
- short story
- songwriting
- playwriting
- graphic novel
- creative non-fiction

For submission details, visit
www.verbaleyze.org

VerbalEyze serves to foster, promote and support the development and professional growth of emerging young writers.

VerbalEyze is a nonprofit organization whose mission is to foster, promote and support the development and professional growth of emerging young writers.

The *Young Writers Anthology* is published as a service of VerbalEyze in furtherance of its goal to provide young writers with access to publishing opportunities that they otherwise would not have.

Fifty percent of the proceeds received from the sale of the *Young Writers Anthology* are paid to the authors in the form of scholarships to help them advance in their post-secondary education.

For more information about VerbalEyze and how you can become involved in its work with young writers, visit www.verbaleyze.org.

www.ingramcontent.com/pod-product-compliance
Lightning Source LLC
Chambersburg PA
CBHW022341040426
42449CB00006B/664